Soul Be Free II

Soul Be Free II

ALFONSO WYATT
and
OUIDA C. WYATT

Soul Be Free II

Copyright © 2014
by Alfonso & Ouida C. Wyatt

cover design by Lucy Swerdfeger

All rights reserved. No part of this book may be used or reproduced in any manner whatsoever without written permission from the publisher, except in the case of brief quotations embodied in articles and reviews.

Published by

The Power of Hope Press
6137 East Mescal Street
Scottsdale, Arizona 85254-5418

ISBN: 978-1-932842-79-1 — $ 12.95

The Power of Hope Press seeks to publish books drawn from actual life experiences that educate, edify, and inspire.

Printed in the United States of America

Soul Be Free II
Preface

Soul Be Free II recognizes that in life it is possible to grow as you go—if that is your desire. It is our intention to build on the insights, wisdom and life truisms found in the first edition of *Soul Be Free: Poems Prose & Prayers*. We are charged to take readers deeper into the paradox of living by delving deeper into the awesome mystery of God. There are so many people caught up in downward spirals, stuck in creative holding patterns; trapped by circumstance; bad decision-making or suffering from being needy and greedy. Traditional therapeutic interventions may deal with problems like: depression, self-loathing, boredom, or family issues from purely a problem-solving perspective. The mission of *SBF II* is to make clear the importance of translating spiritual principles into everyday living.

This book, like the first work, is divided into four sections: The Mind, The Issues, The Relationship and The Soul. The selected poetry, prose and prayers work together to help the reader look beyond the temporal and visible that defines natural circumstance and to glimpse the infinite and invisible that speaks to the supernatural and eternal. There are many people at varying levels of spiritual insight and scriptural knowledge experiencing a hunger to know self and God in a deeper way. It is clear that their needs cannot always be met in traditional or one-size-fits all formats or explanations.

In this present age, far too many people worship what can be seen, touched, idolized or spent. It is important to know that there is another way to live, move and grow. It is not our intention to appear "deep" for deep sake or to promote ourselves as authorities of the spiritual realm. We are yielded vessels who have suffered in order to grow—then share learned life and spiritual lessons. It is our strong desire, as spiritual/life coaches, to assist readers to stop *looking* at personal problems, private hurts, yearning, self-imposed limitations, mistakes, errant thought patterns or missed opportunities and begin to *see* and experience the ever present, life transforming, power of an omnipotent and all loving God.

Deep calls out to deep… Psalm 42:7a

Foreword

Rev. Dr. Andrea M. Hargett

The truth about Jesus's life, death and resurrection – His divine purpose if you will, is powerfully made personal in the poems, prose and prayers of Alfonso and Ouida Wyatt in the second volume of Soul Be Free. Human beings are made in the image of God with the blessed ability to communicate through both written and spoken word. This is a powerful capacity for both good and evil. Words have the potential to create or destroy, to wound or heal, humiliate or encourage. As a wife, mother, teacher, leader and pastor I know too well that words can be used to intimidate, provoke, veto and even stymie destinies. Think about the hurtful words that once penetrated the veneer of your outer shell and deeply punctured your very soul. Too many men, women, boys and girls in our families, congregations, schools and neighborhoods are still suffering from such wounds.

If we ever needed assurance and affirmation, we need it now. Is there any hope? Is there a word to make the broken whole, the anxious calm, the captive free? Yes, there is a word! In a culture engulfed in toxic talk and condemning headlines the writers' proclamations pave a path out of the gloom and doom that paralyzes potential in both individuals and communities. Alfonso and Ouida speak words of life into hurting souls of all generations. People connected to a community of faith or presently disengaged from the church will find a fresh opportunity to encounter the reality of Jesus' love, compassion and wisdom. The authors thought provoking words provide a sanctuary for deep soul searching and reflection.

When read thoroughly the selections engage the intellect, emotion and spirit in ways that broaden and transform our understanding of relationship with God and one another. The reader is wooed to live closer to God and a desire to live in ways that honor the "Soul Liberator." For those willing and ready to give up a dismal worldview and receive a life of freedom and victory, *Soul Be Free II* offers the prescription. The debt owed to these authors for turning their experiences and awareness of pain and sorrow, suffering and sacrifice into poetic medication can only be paid by speaking words of life to ourselves and others because it is clear: "Death and life are in the power of the tongue, and those who love it will eat its fruit." (Proverbs 18:21 NKJV).

Table of Contents

The Mind

level three	1
STRENGTH TO STAND	4
why me	6
MIND RIFF	8
thoughts…	10
FOR THE ASKING	12
The Prayer for the Mind	14

The Issues

big parade	17
SWIFT TRANSITIONS	19
wellspring	21
THIRSTING	23
modern tragedy	25
LISTEN HEAR	27
The Prayer for Issues	29

The Relationship

BEYOND THE SURFACE	33
love lost	35
ANGEL WITH A BROKEN WING	37
song of the nightingale	39
THE MISSION	41
technopoet: obsession (tp 8.0)	43
The Prayer for Relationships	45

The Soul

SOUNDS OF WORSHIP	49
peace haven	51
BLOOD LINES	53
lonely prayer	55
SOUL REFRESH	57
metaphors	59
The Benediction	61
The Scriptures	65-66
About the Authors	67

*Poems in lower case are by A. Wyatt and poems in UPPER CASE are by O.C. Wyatt.

We dedicate this book to the
Spirit
that teaches, mentors,
and guides with grace.

THE MIND

level three
(union)

now for something else
    quite strange
heights and depths
    of reality's range
the world looks
    yet few will see
        divine dimension called level three

                your words peculiar
                can't be true
                why i never heard
                of level two
                what is is that's all
                is can be
            don't you know the truth
                sets you free

darkness can blind
        and so can light
level three demands
        unyielding insight

                this level three
                seem hard to obtain
                naked truth
                we surely disdain
                reality for me
                just like clay
                we all knead to
                have our own way

for those who fail
to persevere
this revelation
      never quite clear
down life's road
find destiny
      in your soul seek level three

Our five senses are a wonderful gift yet each is limited to interpreting the natural world. It is impossible to discern the realm of the supernatural where thought and reason are not always rational and seldom linear without the gift of revelation. Revelation tears away the mental map in the mind and the veil over the eyes so that one can stop looking and start seeing. Revelation takes seekers on a deep inward journey into the depth of the mind and soul where it is possible to come closer to God.

Then the disciples came and asked him, "Why do you speak to them in parables?" He answered, "To you it has been given to know the secrets of the kingdom of heaven but to them it has not been given… But blessed are your eyes, for they see, and your ears, for they hear. Truly I tell you, many prophets and righteous people longed to see what you see, but did not see it, and to hear what you hear but did not hear it.
— Matthew 13:10-11, 16-17 (NSRV)

STRENGTH TO STAND

MY SOUL LOVES THE LORD
HERE AND NOW MY DECLARATION
MAY I TAKE THE PLUNGE
INTO THE PLACE
YOU'VE PREPARED FOR ME

THE ONE YOU HAVE FORGIVEN
BEFORE
I WAS CLEARED
JUST DRIVEN

TO THE PEOPLE, PLACES AND THINGS
OF LIFE THAT LURE
THEN STING

I BOWED AT YOUR FEET
AND SORELY WEPT
HOW DID I ESCAPE
ALL THOSE TRAPS SET

REACHING FOR YOUR OUT-STRETCHED HAND
THERE I FOUND
THE STRENGTH TO STAND
MAKING KNOWN
TO ALL I MEET

MY SOUL LOVES THE LORD
HERE AND NOW MY DECLARATION

Exercising your faith will strengthen you at the core of your being. The more you stand for what you believe the more you can withstand the pitfalls, obstacles, and opposition in life. These roadblocks can never thwart God's plan for you, so keep the faith and run your race.

I will extol the Lord at all times; his praise will always be on my lips. My soul will boast in the Lord; let the afflicted hear and rejoice.
— Psalm 34:1-2

why me

from deep within
the lament born
endless refrain
    why me
        to feel the urge of freedom's song
        sweet aria of the soul then watch
        perfect notes wither and die
    why me
        to daily mourn the corruption of truth
        lustily cheered by celebrants
        their rapture is deceit
    why me
        to see true love
        tragically misshapen
        by artful benders
        once beautiful now grotesque
    why me
        to question injustice when painfully clear
        the game never meant to be won
        just played
        there are no rules
        no constants
    why me
        to yet have faith in tomorrow
        in the great vision of the ancestors
        undeterred by betrayers of the dream

        why me

There is not a person who can truly say that he or she has not uttered "why me?" It is natural to wonder why me, especially when deep and unsettling trouble or a social wrong invades one's private space. Why me cannot be allowed to become a statement of victimhood. When why me is asked introspectively (not accusingly) this probing question can be the key to open a door deep in one's being where the answer can be found.

"I have told you these things, so that in me you may find peace. In this world you will have trouble. But take heart! I have overcome the world."
— *John 16:33*

MIND RIFF

BE NOT CONFORMED
    CHOOSE RENEWING OF THE MIND
        BY NOT RETURNING EVIL IN KIND
            NON-STOP, RE-NEW, BE-NEW,
            FOR HE KNEW
                TRANSFORMED
                    BY THE STORM

How will you renew your mind? There is a choice to be made in how you handle what you encounter. Will you be taken down or lifted up? Taken down by trials, slights, and plots, or lifted up by getting to the hidden treasure in all of life's lessons. Choose to renew daily by counting your blessings.

Do not repay evil with evil or insult with insult, but with blessing, because to this you were called so that you may inherit a blessing.
— *1 Peter 3:9*

                        thoughts…

create >< destroy   pause >< react
liberate ><conquer   adore ><despise
attack><defend   love ><hate
                or
serenely ponder
                        thoughts…
owe no allegiance
and therein
lies the risk
                of
                        thoughts…

invisible power meets
or misses will
not
                all
                        thoughts…
will tear a world asunder
create a new thing
                some
                        thoughts…

are doomed
                to
hurl ideas
toward closed minds
potential unexplored
                wasted
                        thoughts…

I am a thinker. At first thought one may say that is a good thing. I learned the hard way that it is possible to engage in over-thinking. An over-thinker's delight/trap is to weigh ALL conceivable options while simultaneously rethinking what already has been thought long into the night. The over-thinker can become immobilized by simultaneous old and emerging thoughts of: what if, how come, when will or how long? Sometimes we have to get to the place when we tell our mind to shut up.

For I know the thoughts that I think toward you, saith the Lord, thoughts of peace and not evil, to give you an expected end.
— *Jeremiah 29:11KJV*

FOR THE ASKING

PROMISE
PROVISION
VISION
        AN APPOINTED TIME
        KEEP THE FAITH
        FULFILLED IN LIFE
        WALKING WISE
        DREAMS REALIZED
    BUT THERE LURKS
    THE MISCHIEVOUS ONES
  DREAM KILLERS SPIRIT DETRACTORS
  WITH SHOUTS OF ABANDON INSIDE
    JUST EMBELLISH OUTSIDE
BOTTOM FEEDERS
NON-BELIEVERS
GRABBING AND GOING
ALL FOR SHOW
WHO NEXT TO TELL
WHAT I SHOULD KNOW
GRACE IS EVER FLOWING
    FOR THE ASKING
        PROMISE
        PROVISION
        VISION
    AN APPOINTED TIME
    KEEP THE FAITH
    FULFILLED IN LIFE
    WALKING WISE
    DREAMS REALIZED

We've got to walk in the way that has been marked for us. How do we know the way? We know by looking wholeheartedly to the one who knows us best; our Creator God. The gifts, talents, and abilities we have are the rich deposits that can only be optimized in His hand. We have an inheritance and God's grace is sufficient giving direction to our pathway.

And God is able to make all grace abound to you, so that in all things at all times, having all that you need, you will abound in every good work.

— 2 Cor 9:8

A Prayer for The Mind

God let our mind be surrendered to your care. Allow us to observe and absorb love so we can know you all the more. Hear our questions emanating from deep within and let your grace navigate the way so that we may grow stronger, closer and wiser. We pray for patience to hear your still small voice when you speak to our mind and soul. Help us hear the answer to our mind's queries that are revealed through living negotiated by faith. Amen

The Issues

big parade

life the passing parade
goes by
marching tribute a laugh
a sigh
horns with their
shrill blast
find the earnest and
steadfast
drums roll a staccato
beat
pass heads bowed
in defeat
cymbals collide
clashing sound
lifting spirits in
all around
high steppers in
cadence pace
in unity for the
human race
see the parade as
i do
life is marching on
for you

In life's parade there is a continuous passing of good times and bad, happy and sad punctuated by moments of boredom. It is impossible to live and not be part of the parade. Even if you turn your back, run away, close your eyes; if you are laughing or crying the parade will pass you by. Hold fast to this truism: Life moves on no matter what.

We are hard pressed on every side but not crushed; perplexed but not in despair; persecuted, but not abandoned; struck down, but not destroyed.
— *2Cor 4:8-9*

SWIFT TRANSITIONS

AS I LAY ME DOWN TO SLEEP
I PRAY THE
LORD MY SOUL TO
KEEP

I BELIEVE IN THE SECOND COMING
HOWEVER WHO IS REALLY
PREPARED FOR THE
GOING?

TO BE ABSENT FROM THE BODY
SURELY NOT OF MY CHOOSING
JUST LOOKS TOO MUCH
LIKE I'M THE ONE
LOSING

IF I SHOULD DIE
BEFORE I WAKE
I PRAY THE LORD
MY SOUL TO
TAKE

FOR THE NATURAL EYE
BLIND TO WHAT
THE SOUL CAN
SEE
THERE IS PERFECT HEALING
IN BEING SET
FREE.

Life is filled with swift transitions. We are born and will die. We've got to be ready to move from this physical plane. Our true place of rest is in the Savior's arms for truly earth has no sorrow that heaven cannot heal.

So we fix our eyes not on what is seen, but on what is unseen. For what is seen is temporary, but what is unseen is eternal.
— 2Cor 4:18

wellspring

all hail
the well-keeper
master over
shattered dreams
broken promises
the final ceremony
for you made bold by madness
questioning the sanity to move on

                        hear the well-keeper's words
                          true liberation will come
                            through self-destruction
                          my drinkers stay clear of

            the heretics

they struggle for life
finding great strength
in spiritual waters
to put down the cup
their blasphemy

            sip
            and
            believe

Thirst is the strongest bodily urge we have. Does fame and fortune sate your thirst? Has the thirst to be loved no matter what placed you in a compromising position? Do you thirst for revenge after being wronged? It is important to know what is causing your thirst because it can drive you to a place where all is not well.

"Everyone who drinks this water will be thirsty again, but those who drink of the water I will give them will never be thirsty. The water that I will give will become in them a spring of water gushing up to eternal life."

—John 4:13b-14 (NRSV)

THIRSTING

YOU WANT
      TO FEEL THE SPIRIT
    BEYOND THE CHURCH WALLS

YOU WANT
      TO WALK AND BE
  ENCOURAGED NOT DISCOURAGED DAILY

YOU WANT
      THE PUSH OF PURPOSE
      AT YOUR BACK
      INSTEAD OF
    BEING PULLED IN ALL
        DIRECTIONS
    THAT'S WHAT YOU WANT

YOU WANT
      THE SCAB OF PAST
      HURTS HEALED

YOU WANT
      NEGATIVE VOICES
  FROM THE OUTSIDE AND INSIDE
        SILENCED

YOU WANT
      EVERY YEARNING
  YOU'RE THIRSTING FOR QUENCHED
    THAT'S WHAT YOU WANT

            AND GOD WANTS
            YOU TO SAY YES!

It takes courage to look up to God and not our circumstance. Truth is if we don't let go of our growing list of wants, desires, and longings we delay what God has for us. The Almighty One knows the present and the future, so looking to Him first must be the priority.

But seek first his kingdom and his righteousness, and all these things will be given to you as well.

—Matthew 6:33

modern tragedy

this play repeated many a time
so rehearsed walk through
in mime
actors playing out the same routine
while deep down hearts yearn
for a different scene
all movements dictated
by time and space
the invisible directors set the pace
they never hear the sad
cries of woe
their only concern is
the playing of the show
some actors rebel and end their part
high price for taking their
role to heart
others cope by ad-libbing their script
their feet set on a
mind boggling trip
what do you do
in this universal play
where anyone can be
star for a
day

The belief in the power of "most" as in most people are automatically right has created devoted followers of trends, fanatic worshipers of fads and shameless people pleasers. Their seemingly confident walk can create a sense of movement but closer scrutiny reveals there is no significant distance traveled; no lasting lessons learned; just the hapless crowd acting, shouting, planning, networking, dating, moving but never quite managing to arrive to a satisfying place. So the play starts all over picking up new actors along the way mouthing the same old tired words. Beloved, learn how to disbelieve so that you can believe.

How long will you simple ones love your simple ways? How long will mockers delight in mockery and fools hate wisdom?
— Proverbs 1:22

LISTEN HEAR

WHAT IS IT ABOUT LISTENING
THAT I CAN'T HEAR?
HEARING FROM ME
ABOUT ME
SEEMS TO ESCAPE
ME

IS LISTENING AND HEARING
A FADING SKILL
OR AN ACT OF MY
WILL?

LISTEN: MY HEARING
IS BEING DROWNED OUT
BY THE NEW-NOW-NEXT-BEST
WAY OF MULTI-TASKING
WHILE BASKING
IN "DISTRACTEDNESS"

BE STILL
                        WHY SHOULD I?
SMALL VOICE
                  FROM WITHIN WHERE?
CALLING OUT
                  TO AND
                  THROUGH WHOM?
TODAY
                  I LISTEN
                  AND HEAR!

There are times when you hear things while trying to listen to something else. It's hard to hear when the loudness of "now-ness" demands our attention. We have commentary on the latest this or that but how do we really feel? Beloved words from on high come to you in the stillness of your being, and there is no need to fear what you will hear.

"Be still, and know that I am God; I will be exalted among the nations, I will be exalted in the earth."

— Psalm 46:10

The Prayer for Issues

God give us the ability, we pray, to be spirit informed by a dimension greater than our circumstance. There is nothing we have gone through you do not know about and your mighty hand can deliver from all that we experience in our earthly walk. Help us to elevate in our understanding Oh God, empower us to look up then reach up for our divine restoration. Be with us as we learn to close our natural eyes in order to see in the Spirit. Amen.

The Relationship

BEYOND THE SURFACE

HOW DO YOU GET
    TO THE DEEP GIFTING
    THE PLACE OF ABANDON
    WHERE EXPRESSION
        IS IDENTITY

            HOW DO YOU GET
    TO THE ROOT OF KNOWING
    WHERE HEARING IS SPECIFIC
      TO THE ONE WHO
        LISTENS

HOW CAN YOU
    FOLLOW WHILE MAKING A PATH
      LIKE THE BRANCHES
      THAT EXPAND
      FROM THE VINE
      THE RELATIONSHIP
        IS BEYOND
        THE SURFACE

The Bible tells us that in all of our getting, get wisdom. In order to experience all that we have been created to do we've got to stay connected to the power source. This is accomplished through praise, worship, and prayers to God The Father. Building on a strong foundation and maintaining this relationship opens the door for mysteries to unfold.

I am the vine; you are the branches. If a man remains in me and I in him, he will bear much fruit; apart from me you can do nothing. If you remain in me and my words remain in you, ask whatever you wish, and it will be given you.

—John 15:5,7

                    love lost

                    precious jewel
                      this gift
                    often squandered
                    as love dies daily
                    only to be reborn
                    in the broken hearted
                    clinging to yesterday's
what if
do you think
just suppose   hopeless options
                       meet shaken faith
                       mournful cries
                       days into night
                       night into days
this last love prayer
                        take my sorrow
                        take my pain
                        to eternity's shore
                     oh the insignificance
                        of insignificance
my love
        your love
                our love
                            all
                    lost in time's womb

The wonderful gift of love is the greatest form of human expression we can offer to another. Many people, if truthful, want to believe in love and be in a lasting loving relationship. That is a nice sentiment and a joy to witness. Please be clear there is more to love than just being in love. The same love people write about, sing and yearn for can turn to hatred when not properly respected, caringly protected or truthfully corrected.

Love is patient, love is kind. It is does not envy. It does not boast. It is not proud. It is not rude. It is not self-seeking. It is not easily angered, it keeps no record of wrongs. Love does not delight in evil but rejoices with the truth. It always protects, always trusts, always hopes, always perseveres. Love never fails...

— 1Cor 13: 4-8a

ANGEL WITH A BROKEN WING

I MET AN ANGEL
WITH A BROKEN WING
AT FIRST IT SEEMED
THE STRANGEST THING
                        A MESSENGER DOWN
                           WITH ONE WING

        HE KEPT ON MOVING AROUND
                AS HE SHARED
            I COULD SEE JUST
        WHY I'D COME THIS WAY
  WITH ME THE HEALING BALM TO APPLY
          THESE WORDS TO SAY

GOD IS IN YOUR MIDST
NO NEED TO FEAR
HE CAN SEE YOU AND HEAR YOU,
HE FELT YOU LAND HERE

        THERE OUT OF THE BLUE
        IN SERVICE TO ANOTHER
    THE ANGEL WITH A BROKEN WING
          SOON WOULD DISCOVER

                NO ERRORS IN GOD
              NO MISTAKES INDEED
          THE POWER OF PRESSING
            BY FAITH HEALING ME

God always has a way of letting us know that we are on his mind. Just when we are ready to throw in the towel someone speaks a word that goes direct to the heart of the matter. It is in these moments we realize that truly God is closer than our very breath.

Who shall separate us from the love of Christ? Shall trouble or hardship or persecution or famine or nakedness or danger or sword?
— Romans 8:35

song of the nightingale

who dares seek
        perfection
you
        the lovers of contradiction
        blinded by your quest
        to be proven right
                well here i am
                      in:
        the nightingale's song of her soul
        sunset colors from the master's palette
        true love the perfect inspiration
                          yet
                          there is danger in the
                          natural pursuit
            ask those
        driven to distraction
        chasing images
perfect
        in their elusiveness
                never
                      to
            hear the nightingale's song
            be one with the setting sun
            give their love to another

I know people who are perfectionists. There is nothing wrong with wanting to do things right. However, perfectionists seek to go beyond what is right in search of what is perfect. This person can become physically, mentally and spiritually immobilized by the demand to do what is perfectly impossible. There is good, better and best but there is no perfection down here.

"My grace is sufficient for you, for my power is made perfect in weakness."
— 2Cor 12:8b

            THE MISSION

POET
PREACHER
TEACHER
REACHER
            CAPTURE WHAT I'M
                THINKING
                    SAYING
                        PRAYING

                AT THE CORE
            GOD IS TRIUMPHANT
            OVER ALL ADVERSITY
              GREAT AND SMALL

              SHED SOME LIGHT
              ON YOUR MIDNIGHTS
              'CAUSE YOUR STAND
                MEANS I CAN

                THE MISSION

                                POET
                            PREACHER
                            TEACHER
                            REACHER
        SPEAK TO THE CONDITION
            OF BEING HUMAN

In order to lift as we climb we've got to share our story. Letting others know what you've been through makes us human. It is through our humanity that hope is built up and faith can stand strong. Transparent communication is the imperative in this day and time. The clarion call for truth has gone forth, will you answer today?

How, then can they call on the one they have not believed in and how can they believe in the one of whom they have not heard? And how can they hear without someone preaching to them?
— Romans 10:14

technopoet:obsession
(tp 8.0)

words
2 soothe
your broken heart
2 kindle a spark
when u need light
2 give credence
2 the incomprehensible
when u are 2 confused
or need the right word
2 take flight in fantasy
or 2 address ur life off screen
my vow 2 b there
4 ever
& a day :>
even n future
versions of me
4 I know you will
4 ever b
waiting
yearning
searching
4 completion n me
xoxo

Please do not take this as a technophobe's rant. It is time to take a critical look at what or who takes up our time or saps our strength. As a student of life it is clear that technology occupies an increasing growing space in our daily routines and social interactions. So much so social networks may take precedence over real and dynamic social relationships. The incessant and habit forming demand for attention our new and ever improving (and shrinking) devices call for make us seemingly omnipresent by not being present. This is a high price to pay, namely, to be simultaneously connected and disconnected.

In the beginning was the Word, and the Word was with God and the Word was God. He was in the beginning with God. All things came into being through him and without him not one thing came into being. What has come into being in him was life and the life was the light of all people. The light shines in the darkness, and the darkness did not overcome it.

—John 1:1-5 NRSV

The Prayer for Relationships

We petition you for the desire and power to thoroughly examine our relationship to people, to places and to things. As we uncover the motivation behind each we will discover that keeping you at the forefront will enable us to maintain perspective and balance. We pray that as we move closer to you we will recover from filling up on the cares of this world—and still being empty! Thank you for showing us what unconditional love looks and feels like; may we go forth and evidence this love to our brothers and sisters and to self. Amen.

The Soul

SOUNDS OF WORSHIP

WORSHIP IS THE AWESOME SOUND OF
OPEN HEARTS FROM ALL AROUND

JOIN WITH SEEKERS SOARING HIGH
SOULFUL SIRENS TOUCH THE SKIES

LORD MEET US AT THE POINT OF NEED
AS WE SOW OUR MUSTARD SEED

WINDS OF WORSHIP WAVES OF WORSHIP
SWEET SOUNDS OF WORSHIP DRAW ME NEAR

WORSHIP IS THE AWESOME SOUND THAT
PICKS ME UP WHEN I FEEL DOWN

WANDERING THROUGH LIFE'S TERRAIN
FEELING BROKEN AND IN PAIN

LOOKING TO THE HILLS ABOVE
REMINDED OF YOUR ENDLESS LOVE

WINDS OF WORSHIP WAVES OF WORSHIP
SWEET SOUNDS OF WORSHIP DRAW ME NEAR.

It is in the worship that we seal our relationship to The Creator. It is in the worship that there is a breaking in the atmosphere between heaven and this earthly plane. It is the place where God pours into his children and we find strength to go on. And it is in the assembly of worshippers beloved, that the anointing is palpable and where we find liberation for souls that are bound.

Come let us bow down in worship, let us kneel before The Lord our Maker; for he is our God and we are the people of his pasture, the flock under his care.

— Psalm 95:6-7

peace haven

                wings be strong
soar my soul
    above waters of confusion
    beyond the shore of narcissism
    depth for unconcern
    unfathomable
    desire for fame insatiable
                wings be strong
fight storms of adversity
    dark clouds ahead
    ominous shadow of fate
                wings be strong
peace haven over the rise
    love in silent sharing
    snared by earthbound cares
    never to fly again
                wings be strong
rest the constant temptation
    must take to the air
    in unison our cry
    lost in the wind
                wings be strong

It is possible to believe in God yet still want to give up when tested. As long as there is breath in the body there will be adversity that can weaken our resolve. With that said, trials and tribulation in life must be expected. If you feel weary and heavy laden, take your rest, utter a resolute prayer, then keep on keeping on…

Do you not know? Have you not heard? The Lord is the everlasting God, the Creator of the ends of the earth. He will not grow tired or weary and his understanding no one can fathom. He gives strength to the weary and increases the power of the weak. Even youths grow tired and weary and young men stumble and fall but those who hope in the Lord will renew their strength. They will soar on wings like eagles; they will run and not grow weary, they will walk and not be faint.

— Isaiah 40:28-31

BLOOD LINES

WHAT LURKS DEEP IN THE DNA?
EXPRESSIONS UNMASKED
BY THE ANCESTORS PAST
WATCHING, MOVING
TRYING TO SEE
WHAT MY LIFE CHOICES
REVEAL ABOUT ME

WHAT LURKS DEEP IN THE DNA?
EMOTIONS CLINGING JUST LIKE A RASH
EACH CHANGE OF MOOD
SHOWING IN SHARP CONTRAST
WHO'S TO BLAME
WHILE LIVING THE SHAME
OF SOMEONE ELSE'S WOE
WHILE TRYING TO DROWN OUT THE SHOUTS
YOU'RE JUST LIKE SO-AND-SO

WHAT LURKS DEEP IN THE DNA?
ALL STRENGTH AND WILL AND TENACITY
COMES FROM THE BLOOD THAT WAS
SHED BY THE CRUCIFIED ONE

NOW SEEING BEYOND
A BLEAK HORIZON
THE DEBT FOR SIN
PAID BY
HIS RISING

No matter who your birth parents are; no matter what came down through your family line; no matter how you feel about it—there is a soul liberator. Jesus died so that we can be free of any and all bondage. Receive him today and walk into your inheritance.

But the plans of the Lord stand firm forever, the purposes of his heart through all generations.
— Psalm 33:11

lonely prayer

alone so all alone
    life's flame
    she flickers as she dance
    near last wind
    all must succumb
alone so all alone
    waiting
    watching
    wishing
    eyes pierce the sky
    there are no more tears
    and no tomorrows
    only the moment when
alone so all alone
    darkness caress this pain
    solo rage
    tempest in my soul
alone so all alone
    yet now i hear
    faint whisper
    peace be still

                                        alone
                                      no more
                                      my child

What I know about life is that there will come a time when loneliness can be one's only companion. It is quite possible to be in a crowd and still feel lonely. It is important to differentiate being alone and lonely. One may be alone by choice which is different from being lonely by circumstance. Being alone can allow for introspection but being lonely can turn the same enlightening thoughts into subjective accusations.

When my spirit grows faint within me it is you who know my way... Look to my right and see; no one is concerned for me. I have no refuge; no one cares for my life. I cry to you, O Lord; I say, "You are my refuge, my portion in the land of the living." Listen to my cry, for I am in desperate need;...

— Psalm 142:3a, 4-6a

SOUL REFRESH

SOUL REFRESH:
>PRAISE AND WORSHIP
>PRAYER, REFLECTION

INTERNAL SCREEN SAVER:
>MINUTE ESCAPES TO PARADISE
>PROPELLED TOWARD NEW HEIGHTS
>FOCUSED ON BEAMS OF LIGHT

DIVINE DEFAULT:
>CALM AT THE CORE
>LAMENT NO MORE

Taking time during the day to focus on praising God for what He has done will help us stay centered. Worshiping God for who He is in our life is what we were created to do. Lifting His name takes our spirit out of the ordinary into the extraordinary movement of God's plan for our lives.

May the words of my mouth and the meditation of my heart be pleasing in your sight, O Lord, my Rock and my Redeemer.
— Psalm 19:14

metaphor

as the flower
    toils and spins
    seemingly frail roots
    can pierce a stone heart

as the wind
    move the air
    part clouds of deception
    the gift revealed
    glorious light

as the snowflake
    heart so pure
    innocence unquestioned
    free from sullied hands

as the sword
    destroys the web
    tangling our souls
    we petition your name
                      come
                          find
                              us
                                  oh
                                        truth

Jesus used parables as a teaching tool to explain the mysteries of the Kingdom of God. Through common everyday references: a mustard seed, a lost coin, or fig tree, knowledge is gained through the observation of shared experiences. Beloved, aspire to attain the gift of revelation because it allows you to see what God sees.

"...See how the lilies of the field grow. They do not labor or spin. Yet I tell you that not even Solomon in all his splendor was dressed like one of these. If that is how God clothes the grass of the field which is here today and tomorrow is thrown into the fire, will he not much more clothe you...?"

— Matthew 6: 28b-30b

The Benediction

The Benediction

Hear my words as I seek promised refuge in you. I am worn out, done in by the voices I hear pushing and pulling me to places and spaces that I know are not good for me even as I fight to resist. Take me to the place, away from familiar routine and habit—to the place where your deep stream of wisdom, love, peace and contentment freely flows. I need rest from the swirling vortex of this world where discouraging winds attempt to take my eye off of my path, away from my purpose so that I may lose sight of my destiny. Speak to my heart, counsel my mind and soothe my soul. Encourage me Lord. Let me hear in this present silence your still small comforting voice that can pierce the latest greatest clamor of the day. Help me peer into the supernatural realm where your Glory dwells, where truth triumphs and love reigns supreme. Give me Revelation O God so I can stop looking and start seeing you in every aspect and facet of life. Send your healing balm to mentally, physically and spiritually address past hurts, yes, even generational curses. Lift me to heights unknown and to unfathomable depths within my being. Refresh my soul, hear my prayer; give me the will and power to stand as I press toward the mark of the high calling. Allow the fear of the journey and the need for certainty to pass over for I now know: There is no light without you. There is no completeness without you. There is no destiny without you. Hear my words as I seek promised refuge in you. Amen

SCRIPTURES
from the NIV Bible
unless otherwise indicated

THE MIND

PSALM 34:1-2
JOHN 16:33
1 PETER 3:9
JEREMIAH 29:11 (KJV)
2 CORINTHIANS 9:8

THE ISSUES

2 CORINTHIANS 4:8-9
2 CORINTHIANS 4:18
JOHN 4:13b-14 (NRSV)
MATTHEW 6:33
PROVERBS 1:22
PSALM 46:10

THE RELATIONSHIP

JOHN 15:5,7
1 CORINTHIANS 13:4-8a
ROMANS 8:35
2 CORINTHIANS 12:8b
ROMANS 10:14
JOHN 1:1-5 (NSRV)

THE SOUL

PSALM 95:6-7
ISAIAH 40:28-31
PSALM 33:11
PSALM 142:3a, 4-6a
PSALM 19:14
MATTHEW 6:28a-30b

Photo credit: Theodore Coln

REV. DR. ALFONSO WYATT is a renowned public theologian, role model, mentor and national speaker on issues that impact children, youth, families and community health. He is an advisor to government, universities, public schools, community-based organizations and civic groups. He is an Ordained Elder on the ministerial staff of The Greater Allen AME Cathedral of New York where he has designed innovative workshops and seminars for church leaders, men, youth ministries and married couples. Alfonso Wyatt attended Howard University, Columbia Teachers College, The Ackerman Institute for Family Therapy, Columbia Institute for Nonprofit Management, and New York Theological Seminary, serving as an adjunct professor, program advisor and member of the New York Theological Seminary's Board of Trustees. The title of Dr. Wyatt's latest book is *Mentoring From the Inside Out: Healing Boys, Transforming Men*.

You shall receive power when the Holy Ghost comes upon you...

OUIDA WYATT is a Psalmist, artist and writer on the ministerial staff of The Greater Allen AME Cathedral of New York. She has served as an advisor, speaker and facilitator for Chosen Vessels Girl's Rite of Passage, The Cancer Support Ministry and Marriage Enrichment Ministry. Ouida Wyatt designed and taught a course titled *The Power of the Pen: Spiritual Growth Through Journaling*. She is a graduate of the College of New Rochelle, with a B.A. in Psychology. Ouida Wyatt states that her ministry is helping people discover inner peace, power and happiness through a deeper relationship with God and self. Alfonso & Ouida are partners in marriage and ministry for 39 years.

For we have this treasure in earthen vessels...

Notes

Notes

Notes

Notes

Notes

Notes

www.ingramcontent.com/pod-product-compliance
Lightning Source LLC
Chambersburg PA
CBHW022108040426
42451CB00007B/179